UNIVERSITY OF NORTH CAROLINA
STUDIES IN THE ROMANCE LANGUAGES AND LITERATURES

Number 116

THE TEACHINGS OF SAINT LOUIS

THE TEACHINGS OF SAINT LOUIS

A CRITICAL TEXT

BY

DAVID O'CONNELL

CHAPEL HILL
THE UNIVERSITY OF NORTH CAROLINA PRESS

DEPÓSITO LEGAL: V. 604 - 1972

ARTES GRÁFICAS SOLER, S. A. — JÁVEA, 28 — VALENCIA (8) — 1972

For Jewel and Warden

TABLE OF CONTENTS

	Pages
INTRODUCTION	11
THE THREE VERSIONS	13
MEDIEVAL TESTIMONY	16
CRITICAL CONTROVERSY	20
TEXTUAL ANALYSIS	30
THE *Noster* MANUSCRIPT	40
DATE OF COMPOSITION	46
SOURCES	50
TEXT OF THE TEACHINGS	55
VARIANTS	61
BIBLIOGRAPHY	65

INTRODUCTION

It has often been said that one of the interesting sidelights of Joinville's *Vie de saint Louis* is the fact that it contains an edition of Louis' *Enseignements* to his son and successor Philippe III. It is less often noted, however, that the Teachings of Saint Louis contained in Joinville's *Vie* are spurious, having in fact no relationship to the short set of moral guidelines that Louis imparted to his son before he died.

When Natalis de Wailly edited Joinville's *Vie de saint Louis*[1] a little over a century ago, he was convinced that the *Enseignements* that Joinville had included in his biography of the king were authentic. Subsequently, a controversy developed among several scholars, including de Wailly, regarding their authenticity and, as late as 1955, André Artonne,[2] pointing out that the critical treatment of the problem had continued to remain inconclusive, called for a "mise au point définitive" to clear up the questions that still surrounded the various texts of the Teachings.

The aim of the present study is to provide such a "mise au point définitive" in order to establish once and for all which of the three families of texts reproduces most faithfully the *Enseignements de saint Louis*, and to determine whether any member of that group can claim authenticity, including the question as to whether or not one of the various texts might even represent the holograph of Saint Louis. The method used will be both

---

[1] Jean de Joinville, *Histoire de saint Louis, Credo et Lettre à Louis X*, ed. Natalis de Wailly, Paris, 1867.
[2] André Artonne, "Le Recueil des traités de Charles V," *Recueil de travaux offerts à Clovis Brunel*, I (Paris, 1955), 62.

historical and analytical: the former when dealing with the critical controversy surrounding the texts; the latter when studying and comparing the texts themselves. The purpose of this analysis, of course, is to serve as both an introduction to and an argument for the authenticity and historicity of the critical text of the *Enseignements* to be presented here. [3]

---

[3] The publication cost of the present study has been supported in large part by a grant from the Research Council, University of Massachusetts, Amherst.

THE THREE VERSIONS

There are three separate families, or versions, of the *Enseignements de saint Louis*. These three versions may be referred to as the *short version*, the *long version* and the *interpolated version*.

1. The *short version* of the Teachings is represented by the following texts:

   a. Geoffrey of Beaulieu's Latin text, Bibliothèque Nationale, manuscrit latin 13778, printed in *Recueil des Historiens des Gaules et de la France (RHGF)*, XX, 8-9.

   b. A French translation of the Beaulieu text found in the following manuscripts: Bibliothèque Sainte-Geneviève ms. 1273; B.N., ms. fr. 22921; B.N., ms. fr. 916 (copy of 22921).

   c. The Latin text of William of Nangis based on Beaulieu's Latin text, found in the following manuscripts: B.N., ms. fr. 4978; B.N., ms. fr. 23277; printed in *RHGF*, XX, 458, 460.

Among the short versions there are several texts which are exact translations of Beaulieu's prototype except for their omission of one brief paragraph calling on Philip to be loyal to the Pope. These texts are:

   d. The French text by Primat, printed in *RHGF*, XXIII, 59-61.

   e. The French text by William of Nangis in *RHGF*, XX, 459, 461.

f. The text discovered by Gerard of Montaigu in 1374 in the *Trésor des chartes,* now conserved in Registre AA4, Bibliothèque Municipale d'Amiens; printed in *Annuaire-Bulletin de la Société de l'Histoire de France,* (December 10, 1839), 4-8.

  g. The anonymous French text appended to Beaulieu's Latin biography of Saint Louis: B.N., ms. fr. 13778; printed in *RHGF,* XX, 26-27.

2. The *long version* is represented by three groups:

    a. The French text by William of Saint Pathus found in the following manuscripts: B.N., ms. fr. 5722; B.N., ms. fr. 4976; B.N., ms. fr. 5716; printed in *RHGF,* XX, 84-86; the *Vie de saint Louis,* ed. Delaborde, Paris, 1899, 64-71.

    b. The three so-called *Noster* texts, the oldest of which was copied into the *Noster* register of the *Chambre des comptes* by order of Charles V. These three French texts are found in the following manuscripts: B.N., ms. lat. 12814; B.N., ms. fr. 5869; B.N., ms. fr. 4641^b. These two latter texts are copies of 12814. Printed in Adam Théveneau, *Les préceptes du roy saint Louis à Philippe III son fils...* Paris, 1627, 534; Moreau, *Discours sur l'Histoire de France,* XX (1788), 3; Bibliothèque de l'Ecole des Chartes (BECh), LXXIII (1912), 254-262; Emile van Moé, *Les Enseignements de saint Louis,* Paris, 1944.

    c. The Latin text by Yves of Saint Denis, printed in *RHGF,* XX, 45-47.

There are also two hybrid printed editions of the long version.

    d. Paul Viollet, *Œuvres chrétiennes des familles royales de France,* Paris, 1870, 106; based on *Noster* and Saint Pathus.

    e. Natalis de Wailly, "Mémoire sur Joinville et les Enseignements de saint Louis," *Mémoires de l'Acadé-*

mie des Inscriptions, XXVIII (1874), 313-333. This text represents an attempt to reconstitute Saint Louis' original by mixing all three versions.

3. The *interpolated version* differs from the first two in that though it is apparently based on the short version, it both adds several paragraphs and omits the paragraph on the Pope.

    a. This version is found in all three Joinville manuscripts: B.N., ms. fr. nouv. acq. 6273; B.N., ms. fr. 10148. It is also printed in the two early editions of Joinville which are based on lost manuscripts: Antoine-Pierre Rieux, *Chronique et Vie du roi Saint Louis,* Poitiers, 1561; Claude Ménard, *Histoire du Roy Saint Louis,* Paris, 1617. Also printed in Natalis de Wailly's edition of Joinville: *Histoire de saint Louis,* Paris, 1867, 400-405.

    b. An interpolated version can be found in the following texts of the *Grandes Chroniques de France*: B.N., ms. fr. 2615; B.N., ms. fr. 2610; B.N., ms. fr. 1136; B.N., ms. fr. nouv. acq. 4338; Bibliothèque Royale de Bruxelles 10406. Two different texts of this version are printed in *Les Grandes Chroniques de France,* ed. Jules Viard, VII (1932) 277-280, X (1953) 183-186. For further reference to other extant *Grandes Chroniques* manuscripts, see Henri Omont, *Catalogue général des manuscrits français,* [Ancien Supplément Français] III, Nos. 13091-15369 du fonds français, Paris, 1896; [Ancien Petit Fonds Français] III, Nos. 25697-33264 du fonds français, Paris, 1897; [Ancien Saint-Germain Français] III, Nos. 18677-20064 du fonds français, Paris, 1900.

MEDIEVAL TESTIMONY

The first important surviving testimony regarding Louis' Teachings comes from Geoffrey of Beaulieu who for twenty years was Saint Louis' confessor. Two years after the king's death in 1270, Pope Gregory IX called upon Beaulieu to compose a biography of his former spiritual charge. Geoffrey complied with the request and sometime before his own death in 1275 he had completed his task. The work, written in Latin, is short in comparison with the other biographies of the king, but, in the concluding section, Geoffrey begins his version of the Teachings of Saint Louis to Philip with the following statement:

> Caeterum, in finem praesentis capituli supponere dignum duxi, qualiter pater catholicus, quasi Domino revelante, propriae mortis praescius, ante suam infirmitatem extremam scripsit in Gallico manu sûa salutaria documenta, et catholica instituta, quae filio suo primogenito, et in ipso caeteris liberis quasi pro testamento reliquit. Horum documentorum manu sûa scriptorum post mortem ipsius ego copiam habui, et sicut melius et brevius potui transtuli de Gallico in Latinum, quae documenta sunt haec. [1]

Thus, Geoffrey emphasizes that Saint Louis wrote the Teachings intended for Philip in his own hand, in French, and that the version he has recorded is an abbreviation of a copy of the original which he had seen.

---

[1] Geoffrey of Beaulieu, *Vita et Sancta Conversatio Piae Memoriae Ludovici quondam Regis Francorum*, in *Recueil des Historiens des Gaules et de la France*, ed. Bouquet (Paris, 1840), XX, 8. This collection of medieval sources will hereafter be referred to as *RHGF*.

Sometime between December 4, 1302 and October 11, 1303, William of Saint Pathus, who for eighteen years (1277-1295) had been the confessor of Marguerite, Saint Louis' widow, and of their daughter, Blanche, composed, upon the request of the latter, a biography of the saintly king. The work, written in French, is divided into two parts: the first recounts Saint Louis' life while the second describes the miracles performed after his death on behalf of people who invoked his name in their prayers.

The text of the Teachings recorded by William of Saint Pathus is based on the lost Vatican documents emanating from the canonization investigation which was completed in 1297. It differs in two ways from those recorded thirty years earlier by Geoffrey of Beaulieu. The latter had recorded only the Teachings to Philip, whereas Saint Pathus also gives the Instructions to Isabelle. [2] Moreover, Saint Pathus' version is almost twice as long as his predecessor's, not only recording more ample versions of all the paragraphs to be found in Beaulieu's text, but also including some paragraphs entirely absent from the Beaulieu version. It should be recalled here that Beaulieu has confessed to reproducing a version of the Teachings in a fashion both *melius et brevius*, [3] i.e., as well as he could while abbreviating. We shall return to this point when discussing the degree of authenticity of the various versions.

Several years after Saint Pathus had completed his *Vie de saint Louis*, Queen Blanche requested John of Joinville to write a biography of the late king. Joinville had refused to follow Saint Louis to Tunis on the Eighth and last Crusade during which expedition Saint Louis died (1270), but had previously accompanied him on the Seventh Crusade to the Middle East (1248-1254) where he had known him well. Joinville's *Vie de saint Louis* was completed in 1309 and formally presented to Saint Louis' great-grandson, Louis X.

---

[2] The Instructions to Isabelle will not be studied here because they pose a separate and distinct problem, albeit not nearly as complex as those surrounding the texts of the Teachings to Philip. The best available text of the Instructions is to be found in the *Vie de saint Louis* by William of Saint Pathus.

[3] Beaulieu in *RHGF*, XX, 8.

Joinville's text also includes a version of the Teachings to Philip, but his version is a reproduction of neither Geoffrey of Beaulieu's shorter text (1272), nor of William of Saint Pathus' longer one (1302-1303). On the contrary, it strikes a medium between the two extremes and contains paragraphs found in neither of the other two versions. In concluding his work Joinville disclaims all responsibility for the authenticity of whatever he records to which he was not an actual eye-witness. He mentions that he borrowed considerably from a *romant,* and cannot vouch for the historicity of his source. The *romant* to which Joinville refers and which provided him with his version of the Teachings to Philip is probably one of the many manuscripts of the *Grandes Chroniques de France.*

Only some sixty-five years after Joinville terminated his biography, in 1374, Gerard of Montaigu, secretary to King Charles V, discovered in the *Trésor des chartes* a French text of the Teachings to Philip modeled upon Geoffrey of Beaulieu's short version and accompanied by a copy of the Instructions to Isabelle which closely resembled William of Saint Pathus' earlier text. Montaigu passed the manuscript on to Charles V, but before doing so he had a copy made of it to which he attached the following note:

> L'original de ces Enseignements lequel estoit escript d'une grasse lectre qui n'estoit pas trop bonne, fut trouvé par moy, Gerart de Montagu, secrétaire du Roy, au trésor de ses privilèges, chartes et registres dont j'étoie garde; et le baillay au Roy en sa cour du bois de Vincennes, l'an mil IIIc LXXIIII, lequel le baill (bailla) lors à monseigneur le duc de Bourbon frère la Royne, lesquelz estoient descendus du Roy sainct Loys dessusd. et me commanda le Roy que j'en retenisse autant pour garder en son dit trésor.[4]

Gerard of Montaigu must have concluded then that the manuscript which he had found written *d'une grasse lectre* (obviously not the hand of a trained scribe) was in fact the holograph of Saint Louis. It is also probable that Charles V

---

[4] M. Dusevel, "Les Enseignements de saint Louis à son fils," *Annuaire-Bulletin de la Société de l'Histoire de France,* Dec. 10, 1839, p. 7.

agreed, since he presented the text to his brother-in-law Louis of Bourbon and, to our knowledge, in no way gave Montaigu any reason to believe that his interpretation was wrong. Nevertheless, it must be stressed here that the version which Montaigu took for the original belongs to the same family as the version of Geoffrey of Beaulieu who, we recall, stated that his text was merely an abbreviated translation of an original written in French by Saint Louis. Curiously enough, after 1374, the authenticity of the various manuscripts of the Teachings of Saint Louis was not to be discussed again until the end of the nineteenth century.

The teachings of Philip are therefore represented by three different versions: 1) Geoffrey of Beaulieu's shorter version which, according to its author, is an abbreviated Latin translation of the original, and of which the text discovered by Gerard of Montaigu can only be a retranslation into French; 2) the long version of William of Saint Pathus which has a semi-official stamp of authenticity in that Saint Pathus' source material was the official record of the canonization inquest which had been sent to him by the Vatican, and; 3) Joinville's version, a text related to neither previously mentioned tradition, but rather derived, in Joinville's words, from a *romant* which, as we shall shortly see, was in all likelihood one of the many manuscripts of the *Grandes Chroniques de France*. Since the Middle Ages, other texts of the three basic versions of the Teachings to Philip have been discovered, so that in attempting to establish whether any of the three versions represents the holograph of Saint Louis, or, if this is not possible, which offers the highest degree of authenticity, we will have to examine all these texts.

It is worthwhile recalling here that there are actually three extant manuscripts containing Saint Pathus' text of the Teachings, as well as three *Noster* texts. Thus, for the sake of clarity and consistency, the phrase "Saint Pathus text" should be taken to mean the critical text published by Delaborde in his 1899 edition of Saint Pathus' *Vie de saint Louis* and the phrase "*Noster* text" should be taken to mean B.N., ms. lat. 12814.

CRITICAL CONTROVERSY

The problem of deciding the authenticity of the various manuscripts of the Teachings of Saint Louis and, concomitantly, whether any of them actually represents the holograph of Saint Louis, was first studied by Paul Viollet in 1869.[1] According to Viollet the texts of the Teachings can be divided into two separate and easily recognizable groups: those which contain a long version *(texte ample)* and those which contain a short one *(texte bref)*.

The long version is represented by three different texts, one in Latin, the others in French. Viollet attributed the Latin text to a monk from the Abbey of Saint Denis near Paris, who has since been identified as a friar named Yves. Of the two French texts, one had been conserved in the *Noster* register of the *Chambre des comptes* and was designated by Viollet as manuscript A, while the other, which was known to have been composed by Queen Marguerite's confessor (he was not identified as William of Saint Pathus until 1899), was designated as manuscript B.

The short texts were all grouped under the rubric C, and at the head of the list we find Geoffrey of Beaulieu's Latin text. Viollet bunched most of the manuscripts listed on pages 13-15 together in the same family, concluding his entire classification with the following remark:

> Nous accordons la préférence aux textes A et B; les autres textes, d'une étendue moitié considérable, nous

---

[1] Paul Viollet, "Note sur le véritable texte des Instructions de saint Louis à sa fille Isabelle et à son fils Philippe le Hardi," *Bibliothèque de l'Ecole des Chartes (BECh)*, XXX (1869), 129-148.

semblent porter, çà et là, la trace de divers procédés d'abréviation; nous pensons qu'ils ont subi certaines modifications ou corrections encore reconnaissables. [2]

Viollet then chose to trace back all the short texts to the original Latin one of Geoffrey of Beaulieu, with the exception of the texts contained in Joinville and the *Grandes Chroniques de France* which were less worthy of credibility than the others, he thought, because of paragraphs judged to be interpolations.

Viollet's coping with Joinville is a matter of considerable interest. In his *Vie de saint Louis* (completed in 1309) Joinville inserted a version of the Teachings to Philip that apparently was based on the short version. However, Joinville's text contains modifications and interpolations that actually represent neither the short nor the long versions. In attempting to track down the source of these differences, Viollet referred back to the epilogue of Joinville's *Vie* where, we recall, the author mentions a certain *romant* from which he admits having borrowed some source material concerning Saint Louis:

> Je faiz savoir a touz que j'ay céans mis grant partie des faiz nostre saint roy que je ai veu et oÿ, et grant partie de ses faiz que j'ai trouvez qui sont en un romant, lesquiex j'ai fait escrire en cest livre. [3]

Viollet was the first to point out that the Teachings which appeared in the *Grandes Chroniques de France* contained the same differences and peculiarities as those reproduced by Joinville and that all those additional teachings were of a political, not a moral or religious nature. He therefore concluded that the paragraphs which were found only in the manuscripts of the *Grandes Chroniques* and Joinville, and in no other manuscripts, did not belong to the original version of the Teachings and were to be put aside as interpolations which were probably made sometime between 1285 and 1314 in accordance with the political policies of Philip the Fair.

---

[2] *Ibid.*, p. 135.
[3] Joinville, no. 768, ed. de Wailly (Paris, 1867).

Natalis de Wailly's new critical edition of Joinville's *Vie de saint Louis* is roughly contemporary to Viollet's studies. Since Wailly was convinced of the authenticity of everything that Joinville included in the *Vie*, he naturally defended the Joinville text of Saint Louis' Teachings to Philip against Viollet's attacks.[4] Wailly opened the dispute by saying that the versions of the Teachings to be found in Joinville and the *Grandes Chroniques de France* represented together a completely different tradition and that the political interpolations to be found in these manuscripts were actually quite characteristic of Saint Louis, therefore not additions made at a later date. According to Wailly, the holograph of Saint Louis was secretly stored away in the Abbey of Saint Denis; he argues that it would have been superfluous to bring forth Teachings concerned primarily with the efficient political use of temporal power before a board of inquiry whose purpose was to decide Louis' sanctity. It is only after the canonization, Wailly concludes, that the complete document was released and copied.

Viollet's reply[5] expresses his inability to accept that the texts of Joinville and the *Grandes Chroniques* could give birth at once to the long version, which was presented at the canonization investigation, as well as to the short version upon which it is based. He added that it was not Joinville's fault that the version of the Teachings he recorded is not authentic, since, in their dealings with him, the monks of the Abbey of Saint Denis, one of whose manuscripts served as his model, were most likely acting under orders from higher authority.

But Viollet's second argument, in which he attacked manuscript LF4 of the Bibliothèque Sainte-Geneviève, on which de Wailly had founded all his assertions, was even more convincing. Viollet pointed out that this manuscript was very faulty, being both the shortest and the most verbose of all the manuscripts of the *Grandes Chroniques*. Viollet then went on to introduce a new

---

[4] Natalis de Wailly, "Mémoire sur le *romant* ou Chronique en langue vulgaire dont Joinville a reproduit plusieurs passages," BECh, XXXV (1874), 217-248.

[5] Viollet, "Les Enseignements de saint Louis à son fils," BECh, XXXV (1874), 1-56.

manuscript (B. N., ms. fr. 2615), one that predated the Bibliothèque Sainte-Geneviève manuscript and that corresponded more closely to the Joinville text. He was thus able to prove that the versions of the Teachings recorded by Joinville and the various texts of the *Grandes Chroniques* did not constitute a separate and independent tradition. Subsequent scholarly research has more than vindicated Viollet's position on this point. One may now safely conclude that the text of the Teachings to Philip recorded by Joinville is in fact a copy of one of the many interpolated texts which were in existence at the time. Unfortunately, no one has yet discovered the manuscript which Joinville had copied into his *Vie de saint Louis*.

In 1912, Henri-François Delaborde revived the polemic of 1869-1874.[6] His article generally supported Viollet's view of the interpolated texts against that of Natalis de Wailly. In addition, however, Delaborde brought forth a new thesis regarding both the long and short versions of the Teachings and the texts of the Instructions to Isabelle. All of Delaborde's arguments point to a defense of the short version of the Teachings to Philip which he says is not an abbreviation at all:

> Si l'on veut bien se reporter au passage cité plus haut, on y verra que Geofroi de Beaulieu déclare avoir eu communication de l'original autographe des Enseignements de saint Louis à son fils, "horum documentorum manu sua scriptorum... ego copiam habui," et les avoir traduits du francais en latin, "sicut MELIUS et brevius potui," ce qui ne veut pas dire "en les abrégeant," mais "le mieux qu'il a pu et dans les termes les plus concis."[7]

Believing, for this — in our opinion, incorrect — reason in the text of Geoffrey of Beaulieu, Delaborde goes on to state that Saint Louis must have composed three different texts of the Teachings: a short and a long version for his son Philip and a separate set of Instructions for his daughter Isabelle.

---

[6] Delaborde, "Le Texte primitif des Enseignements de saint Louis à son fils," *BECh*, XLLIII (1912), 73-100.

[7] *Ibid.*, pp. 92-93.

> 1) Des instructions brèves — et non pas abrégées comme on l'a cru jusqu'ici — remises à l'aîné, mais destinées à être communiquées par lui à tous ses frères, dans lesquelles le roi leur donnait des préceptes généraux de vie chrétienne et de gouvernement des fiefs.
>
> 2) Des instructions plus détaillées et disposées un peu différémment, adressées à sa fille Isabelle, reine de Navarre, dans lesquelles il avait inséré plusieurs articles spéciaux concernant la conduite que devait tenir une grande dame.
>
> 3) Des instructions plus détaillées, specialement adressées à Philippe le Hardi, dans lesquelles, reprenant, selon le même ordre, les instructions brèves adressées à l'ensemble de ses enfants, le roi donnait à celles de ces instructions qui concernaient la vie chrétienne et la direction purement morale, la forme développée de celles qui avaient trouvé place dans les Instructions à Isabelle, y modifiait certains articles au point de vue particulier de l'héritier du trône, et y ajoutait même une recommendation sur ses devoirs de chef de famille qui ne pouvait s'adresser qu'à lui seul. [8]

Viollet, however, was unwilling to go quite so far as Delaborde; he specifically rejected Delaborde's interpretation of the word *brevius:*

> Pour moi, je ne prends pas *brevius* au sens littéraire et cherché que vous lui donnez. L'étude des documents eux-mêmes, m'oblige à adopter le sens propre du mot *brevius,* et je rends ainsi qu'il suit la pensée de Beaulieu: "J'ai traduit ces Enseignements au mieux et je les ai abrégés. Voici ces textes (mais en latin et abrégés)." Quant aux mots *et in ipso ceteris liberis,* c'est à mon sens, une réflexion de l'historien, qui voit avec raison en ces Enseignements adressés à l'aîné une source d'édification pour tous les enfants du roi. [9]

Comparing the long and short versions of the Teachings, Viollet shows that the latter is not only an abridgment of the former, but is a faulty one at that, since it contains several contradictions and

---

[8] *Ibid.,* p. 99.
[9] Viollet, "Les Enseignements de saint Louis à son fils; Lettre à M. le comte François Delaborde," *BECh,* LXXIII (1912), 495.

omissions. He reminds us that no medieval chronicler ever referred to two distinct lists of Teachings composed by Saint Louis for his son Philip. On the contrary, all medieval sources agree that he left only one set of Teachings to his son, i. e., either the short or the long version.

Delaborde's answer to Viollet's reservations was conciliatory and thereupon the polemic was terminated. [10]

Thus the first round of critical controversy between Paul Viollet and Natalis de Wailly, concerning the version of the Teachings contained in Joinville and the manuscripts of the *Grandes Chroniques de France,* led to their elimination from serious consideration as direct descendants of Saint Louis' holograph. The second round, this time between Paul Viollet and his erstwhile defender Henri-François Delaborde, who agreed with Viollet that the interpolated texts were spurious but who wanted to put the short text of Beaulieu on an equal footing with the long text, proved that the text of Geoffrey of Beaulieu and all the derivative short texts do not reproduce the holograph of Saint Louis. Viollet's interpretation of Beaulieu's use of *brevius* in describing his version of the Teachings, namely that it meant he had "abbreviated" in Latin the original French text of Saint Louis, is completely convincing. Emphasis must therefore be put on the three texts of the long version: the French text found in the *Noster* manuscript, the Latin text of Yves of Saint Denis, and the French text of William of Saint Pathus.

In 1928 Charles-Victor Langlois attempted to sum up the controversy surrounding the long and short versions by advancing the following explanation. Sometime after the canonization investigation of 1274, the copy room at Saint Denis had at its disposal a long version, which it probably received from the Vatican officials, and a short one modeled on Geoffrey of Beaulieu's text. Some scribes, like Yves of Saint Denis, reproduced the long version while others, like William of Nangis or Primat, reproduced the short one. A third group, namely those monks who were assigned to work on the *Grandes Chroniques de France,* made additions or

---

[10] Delaborde, "Réponse de M. le comte François Delaborde," *BECh*, LXXIII (1912), 502-504.

omissions in their texts according either to their own taste or to a policy dictated to them by higher authority.

After offering this plausible explanation of the genesis of the three versions of the Teachings to Philip, Langlois hesitated to go any further than to state that, with regard to the controversy which had taken place between Viollet and Delaborde, he was in complete agreement with the former and that, though he felt that the long version did contain the essence or spirit of Saint Louis' Teachings, he did not think that it preserved the letter of that work.

Langlois seemed convinced that the long texts of the Teachings, like the short ones, had all passed through a Latin version at one time or another. He therefore saw no sense in attempting to reconstitute a critical text. His modern French translation of the Teachings is prefaced with the following statement:

> Ensuite, il suffit d'en faire connaître le sens dans la langue d'aujourd'hui, puisque, l'original étant perdu, l'echo direct de la voix même de Louis IX, qu'il aurait été intéressant d'entendre, est éteint à jamais. Nos textes en français des Enseignements sont tous des versions de moines et des versions médiocres; ils coïncident peut-être parfois avec l'original perdu mais alors c'est par hasard, et il est impossible de désigner maintenant les endroits où cela s'est produit.[11]

Although Langlois' position went unchallenged at the time, the question was opened up again by Auguste Levillain in 1933. Claiming to see a similarity in language and style between the *Noster* manuscript of the Teachings to Philip and the version of the Instructions to Isabelle contained in the manuscript found by Gerard of Montaigu in the *Trésor des chartes* in 1374, Levillain concluded that the *Noster* manuscript of the Teachings to Philip contained not only the spirit but indeed the letter of the Teachings. As Levillain says:

> Or en 1374, Gérard de Montaigu découvrait dans le *Trésor des chartes* dont il avait la garde, des Enseigne-

---

[11] Charles-Victor Langlois, *La vie en France au moyen-âge*, IV (Paris, 1928), 33-34.

ments de saint Louis à son fils et à sa fille sous la forme de deux documents d'archives, et les prenait l'un et l'autre pour les originaux, bien qu'il notât que les Enseignements à Philippe étaient écrits *d'une grosse lettre qui n'était pas trop bonne.* Comme il n'a pas fait la même réserve pour les Enseignements à Isabelle, il est certain que ceux-ci s'offraient à ses yeux avec tous les caractères de l'authenticité. [12]

According to Levillain, Gerard of Montaigu was convinced that the text of the Instructions to Isabelle which he found in 1374 was authentic. With this as his major premise, Levillain adds a corollary to the effect that there are many resemblances between the Montaigu text of the Instructions to Isabelle and the text of the Teachings to Philip contained in the *Noster* manuscript. Unfortunately, he gives no examples at all to prove his assertion. Consequently he can only conclude that the *Noster* manuscript of the Teachings to Philip faithfully records Saint Louis' holograph, and hence represents not only the spirit, but the letter, of the Teachings.

First of all, Levillain would have one believe that the long *Noster* text of the Teachings of Saint Louis was, until 1296, stored in the *Trésor des chartes* along with the text of the Instructions to Isabelle:

> Cependant, Philippe III, en possession des autographes paternels, n'avait pas le choix des moyens pour en assurer la garde, la *Chambre des comptes* n'existant pas encore: il les avait sûrement, à son retour de la croisade, envoyés ensemble au *Trésor des chartes*. [13]

He also believes that it was after this date that Philip the Fair, in conformity with his political policy toward the Pope, had the long text of the Teachings to Philip removed from the dossier where it was accompanied by the Instructions to Isabelle, and substituted for it a French translation of the abbreviated version of Geoffrey of Beaulieu. He did so, says Levillain, because the

---

[12] Léon Levillain, "Discours presentés à la Société de l'Histoire de France," *Annuaire-Bulletin de la Société de l'Histoire de France,* May 16, 1933, p. 82.

[13] *Ibid.,* p. 83.

Beaulieu text contained one significant omission — the article on the Pope — which calls upon Philip to be obedient to him as to a spiritual father. Levillain then claims that Philip the Fair thought that this short text of the Teachings would gain credence if it were accompanied by the official version of the Instructions to Isabelle which, without being touched up, also omits any reference to the Pope.

> Si donc, vers 1300, on pouvait encore voir les Enseignements du roi a sà fille dans ce dépôt et si les Enseignements à Philippe n'y étaient plus, c'est que ceux-ci avaient éte distraits de leur dossier pour faire place au pseudo-original de 1296. [14]

Thus, Levillain would have us believe that the long version had always been conserved in the royal family and has survived down to our day as the *Noster* manuscript of the *Chambre des comptes*. For Levillain states that precisely because Charles V did possess the holograph of Saint Louis, he had no qualms about giving to his brother-in-law Louis of Bourbon the manuscript which Gerard of Montaigu had brought to him.

As far as Levillain is concerned, the *Noster* manuscript contains the letter of the Teachings of Saint Louis to Philip and the text contained in manuscript AA4 of the Bibliothèque d'Amiens reproduces to the letter the Instructions of Saint Louis to his daughter Isabelle. It is essential to recall here, though, that the only proof which Levillain gives for his conclusions is a putative resemblance between the *Noster* text of the Teachings and the text of the Instructions.

Eleven years later, in 1944, Emile van Moé published a text of the Teachings to Philip in which he took the *Noster* text as his base manuscript. He says that he did so because this manuscript seemed to him to be the best but he does not say why, referring only to the "preuve lumineuse" [15] of Levillain as supporting evidence.

Finally, in 1955, André Artonne brought forth a new manuscript which he had found in the *Recueil des traités de Charles V*.

---

[14] *Ibid.*, p. 83.
[15] Emile van Moé, *Les Enseignements de saint Louis* (Paris, 1944), p. 8.

After indicating the existence of this newly discovered manuscript, which, being nothing more than a French translation of the short Latin text of Geoffrey of Beaulieu, is relatively unimportant, he pointed out that the argument given by Levillain in favor of the authenticity of the *Noster* manuscript did not seem logical to him and that nobody had ever answered Levillain or checked out his conclusions. Artonne then terminated his treatment of the problem by saying that it still required a "mise au point définitive." [16]

Now let us examine the problem once again. It seems evident, first of all, that the case against the short version, not to mention the interpolated one, is closed. There is no need to retrace Paul Viollet's steps, for he has proved beyond a doubt that our interest ought to be focussed on the long version. Let us begin, therefore, by examining the long Latin text of Yves of Saint Denis.

---

[16] André Artonne, "Le Recueil des traités de Charles V," *Recueil de travaux offerts à Clovis Brunel*, I (Paris, 1955), 62.

TEXTUAL ANALYSIS

It was Charles-Victor Langlois who stated in 1928 that since the texts found in William of Saint Pathus and *Noster* are retranslations into French of the Latin text which had been recorded in the canonization documents, the Latin text of Yves of Saint Denis, since it is in Latin, is one step closer to the French original of Saint Louis. Unfortunately, since Langlois does not offer detailed proof for this assertion, we must consider his statement as an assumption rather than as fact. It may be well to take a different tack in approaching the Yves of Saint Denis text. Let us try out a comparative technique involving, first, the short Latin text by Geoffrey of Beaulieu and, secondly, the two long French texts.

Studying these two manuscripts, one notes immediately that in terms of Latin style the Yves text is much inferior to the Beaulieu version. The first paragraph shared by both manuscripts demonstrates the consistent difference in style:

SAINT DENIS   Propter hoc, care fili, doceo te primo, quod tu diligas Deum ex toto corde tuo et de toto posse tuo, quia sine hoc nullus potest.

BEAULIEU   Fili carissime, inprimis te doceo, quod dominum Deum tuum diligas ex toto corde tuo, et ex tota virtute tua; nam sine hoc non est salus.

Geoffrey of Beaulieu's abridged translation is written in good Latin style whereas Yves of Saint Denis' text adopts an awkward Romance word order; after a prepositional phrase and a direct address to the recipient of the Teachings, he writes the verb, followed by the object of the verb and an adverbial modifier. After his opening direct address, however, Geoffrey of Beaulieu first writes his adverbial modifier, then his direct object and finally the main verb of the sentence. Clearly, then, when compared to Geoffrey's, Yves' Latin usage is "unnecessarily" Gallicized.

The dependent clause shows the same pattern; not only does Yves begin with the verb, he also includes — redundantly in Latin — the subject pronoun *tu*. Yves then proceeds to write the direct object *Deum;* his two adverbial phrases — *ex toto corde tuo et de toto posse tuo* — follow. Meanwhile, Beaulieu starts off his dependent clause by writing the direct object first (*dominum, Deum tuum*); the verb follows but there is no redundant subject pronoun, and the two adverbial phrases terminate this part of the clause. Finally, the two adverbial phrases *de toto posse tuo* (Saint Denis) and *ex tuto virtute tuo* (Beaulieu) are different in so far as Saint Denis follows medieval usage in using *de* instead of *ex*, but this cannot be called a Gallicism, and the final clauses *quia sine hoc nullus potest* (Saint Denis) and *nam sine hoc non est salus* tell us nothing since they both mean something different. We recall that Beaulieu abbreviates.

In the second paragraph that the two manuscripts have in common the same pattern once again presents itself:

SAINT DENIS — Quicquam debes te custodire ab omnibus quae credas quod ei debeant displicere. Et specialiter debes habere istam voluntatem, quod tu non faceres peccatum mortale pro aliquo re quae posset contingere, et quod tu permitteres tibi ante, omnia membra scindi, et auferri crudeli martyrio vitam, quam tu scienter faceres mortale peccatum.

BEAULIEU — Item: debes te custodire ab omnibus quae Deo noveris displicere, videlicet ab omni mortali peccato: ita quod prius deberes te permittere omni genere martyrii cruciari, quam aliquod mortale peccatum committere.

Here Saint Denis duplicates the French word order of William of Saint Pathus. Whereas Beaulieu uses a straight infinitive construction (*displicere* in conjunction with *custodire*), Saint Denis borrows the subjunctive used by Saint Pathus in French: *Tu te dois garder a tout ton pooir de toutes choses que tu croiras que li doient desplere.*

The second part of this paragraph is shorter and better written in the Beaulieu text. Though he abbreviates the original, his *videlicet ab omni mortali peccato* remains clear. Saint Denis is obliged to translate his text literally for his Romance syntax is calqued upon a French text similar to that of Saint Pathus: *et especiaument tu dois avoir volenté que tu ne feroies pour nule chose du monde péchié mortel.* Saint Denis' linguistic resemblance to Saint Pathus can be seen also in the last two sections of the paragraph. The two main verbs here, both of which are written as infinitives depending on *deberes* in the Beaulieu text, are put in the subjunctive once again by Saint Denis. Here is the Saint Pathus reading: *et que tu soufferoies avant que touz tes membres te fussent trenchiez et que l'en te tolist la vie par cruel martire, que tu feisses a escient pechié mortel.*

The next paragraph displays similar peculiarities in the Saint Denis text:

> SAINT DENIS   Si dominus noster mittat tibi aliquam sustinere persecutionem vel infirmitatis, vel aliam, tu debes ei regratiari et scire bonas grates, quia debes pensare quod bien meruisti et hoc et plus, si ipse vellet, eo quod parum eum dilexisti et parum ei servivisti, et multa fecisti suae contraria voluntati.
>
> BEAULIEU   Praeterea si tibi dominus aliquam tribulationem habere permiserit, benigne, et cum gratiarum actione debes sustinere: cogitans quod ad bonum tuum proveniat, et quod hoc bene forsitan meruisti.

The Saint Denis text once again follows Romance, and not Latin, word order: the subject precedes the main verb, the indirect object, and the direct object, in that order. On the other hand, the Beaulieu text offers a better Latin reading: first the indirect object, then, in sequence, the subject, the direct object, the dependent infinitive, and, finally, the main verb. The author of the Saint Denis text is without doubt carefully translating a French text. When we compare his text with that of Saint Pathus, it is clear that he is indeed producing a faithful translation of a text very similar to the latter: cf., *Se Nostre-Seigneur t'envoie aucune persecucion ou maladie, ou autre chose, tu le dois soufrir de bonne volenté, et li dois rendre graces et savoir l'en bon gré.*

The rest of the paragraph follows the same pattern: (a) Saint Denis repeats the subject pronoun *tu*, which Beaulieu does not do; (b) Beaulieu uses the present participle *cogitans* followed by two dependent clauses, but Saint Denis prefers a Romance-type clausal construction; (c) furthermore, Saint Denis avoids Beaulieu's classical *cogitare* — his adoption of *pensare* brings him a little closer to the French he was translating. His phrase *si ipse vellet* smacks of French; had he not abridged his text, Beaulieu would have probably used an ablative absolute. The influence upon Saint Denis of a French text is patently obvious: cf., *car tu dois penser que il le fait pour ton bien; et ausi dois tu penser que tu l'as bien deservi, et ce et plus, se il vouloit, pour ce que te l'as pou amé et pou servi, et as fet mout de choses contreres a sa volenté.*

The next paragraph, being the antithesis of its predecessor, has almost exactly the same stylistic faults; but in the last sentence of the Saint Denis text we note a poor Latin translation of Saint Louis' Middle French verb:

> Si dominus noster mittat tibi aliquam prosperitatem ut corporis sanitatem vel aliam, tu debes ei regratiari humiliter, et debes cavere tibi, quod ex hoc pejoreris nec per superbiam, nec per aliud vitium; hoc est enim multum grande peccatum, *guerram* domino nostro *facere* ex donis ipsius.

Saint Denis' *facere guerram* is a crude Gallicism for Saint Louis' *guerroier* as found only in the *Noster* manuscript: cf., *car c'est moult grant pechié de guerroier Nostre Seigneur de ses dons.* Beaulieu, whose Latin is cleaner, realized that this verb had to be rendered by a circumlocution in Latin:

> Insuper, si Dominus tibi prosperitatem quamcumque contulerit, debes ei humiliter regratiari: cavens ne inde fias deterior, sive per unam vanam gloriam, sive quocumque alio modo; quia non debes Deum *impugnare, vel offendere* ex donis suis.

Yves of Saint Denis' literal transcription, *facere guerram*, resembles Saint Pathus' *car c'est mout grant pechié, que faire guerre a Nostre Seigneur pour ses dons meemes*. Saint Denis and Saint Pathus come close here — as on a few other occasions — to suggesting a common source although we cannot say that one is a translation of the other. The four texts read, then, as follows:

NOSTER	car c'est moult grant pechié de guerroier Nostre Seigneur de ses dons
BEAULIEU	quia non debes Deum impugnare, vel offendere ex donis suis
SAINT DENIS	hoc est enim multum grande peccatum, guerram domino nostro facere ex donis ipsius.
SAINT PATHUS	car c'est mout grant pechié, que faire guerre a Nostre Seigneur pour ses dons meemes.

The *Noster* text stands alone in this case, as in so many others, while the Saint Denis and Saint Pathus texts closely resemble each other. We can only conclude that the Saint Denis text imitates a French text whose flavor it attempts to carry over into the Latin. Further comparison of these texts would only serve to reinforce the conclusion that the Saint Denis text, unlike that of Beaulieu, contains numerous Gallicisms which tend to betray its affinities to a putative French model. Continued references to paragraphs not specifically analyzed here would only confirm this conclusion.

In comparing the Latin text of Yves of Saint Denis with the Saint Pathus text, one is struck by the clear relationship these texts display. For if Saint Denis' Latin text is characterized by a Gallic influence, Saint Pathus' French contains many obvious

Latinisms. This is so because, as William of Saint Pathus tells us, his text was taken from the official canonization documents:

> Et en la description des choses que nostre sires touz puissanz a deignié fere par le benoist saint Loys, il m'a semblé que je ne devoie fere force en curieuse et aournee maniere descrire; meesmement comme je ni entende nule chose a mettre ne amenuiser, mès ces choses que jai veues escrire loiaument si com eles sont enquises, escriptes, prouvees et examinees par la court de Romme et aprouvees, pource que eles soient creues plus certainement de toute bonne gent.[1]

In his edition of the *Miracles de saint Louis*,[2] P. B. Fay argues that the *Miracles* and the *Vie de saint Louis*, both of which were composed by William of Saint Pathus, were originally written in Latin. Fay offers some convincing proofs for his assertion and they will not be quarrelled with here, for it is not essential to this study to determine whether Saint Pathus' *Vie* was originally composed in Latin or in French. It should be noted, however, that Saint Pathus undertook his biography of Saint Louis because he had been asked to do so by Saint Louis' daughter Blanche:

> Et comme je me sente non soufisant d'escrire la vie tres digne d'ensivre de ce tres excellent saint, je n'eusse en nule maniere ce essaié ne empris, se le fervent desire de noble dame madame Blanche, fille de cel meesmes glorieus saint Looys, ne m'eust a ce semons, et se a ce meemement ne m'eust contreint la copie de l'enqueste sus la vie juree et sus les miracles du glorieus saint Loys, fete de l'autorité de la court de Romme, el tens de beneuree memoire de nostre tres saint pere Martin quart apostoille de Romme...[3]

Now then, since Saint Pathus undertook his *Vie* at the request of Louis' daughter Blanche, it is highly probable that he wrote it originally in French, not in Latin, for a lady of the French court

---

[1] Saint Pathus in *RHGF*, XX, 61.
[2] William of Saint Pathus, *Miracles de saint Louis*, ed. P. B. Fay (Paris, 1931).
[3] Saint Pathus in *RHGF*, XX, 60.

could expect that the text be written in the language of the court.[4] At any rate, the fact that the existing French Saint Pathus text of the Teachings does contain many Latinisms can be explained either by supposing that Saint Pathus first wrote his *Vie* in Latin and later translated it into French, or by assuming that the *Vie* was composed with the Latin texts of the canonization inquest serving as the direct source.

The important point to be made here is that although these two manuscripts are more closely related than any two others that we have, we cannot be sure of their degree of parentage. For if the Latin text of Saint Denis ultimately represents a poor translation of a French text, just as the French text of Saint Pathus is either a translation of a Latin text or is based on a Latin text, there is simply not enough evidence to permit one to conclude that one of the two texts is a direct translation of the other.

The *Noster* manuscript may be judged superior to the Saint Pathus text because it is free of the abundant Latinisms so characteristic of the latter. In paragraph eight of the *Noster* manuscript one finds the following phrase:

> ...et especialment soies plus en pez et plus ententiz a oroison tant come li cors Nostre Seigneur sera presens a la messe et une piece devant.

Et une piece devant is translated by Yves of Saint Denis or by the scribe whose manuscript Yves copied, by the phrase et *per spatium temporis ante*. Meanwhile, the version in the Saint Pathus text is a direct translation from the Latin: *et encore devant par une espace de temps*. The similarity of the Saint Pathus and Yves texts points to their sharing the same tradition, the Latin one, while the *Noster* manuscript, with its *et une piece devant*, betrays no Latin influence.

The relationship between the Saint Pathus and the Saint Denis texts can be seen once again in paragraph eleven where both manuscripts omit a word certainly written by Saint Louis and recorded by the *Noster* text: *Chiers filz, aies volentiers la com-*

---

[4] James Westfall Thompson, *The Literacy of the Laity in the Middle Ages*, University of California Publications in Education, IX (Berkeley, 1939).

paingnie de bonnes gens avec toy. The omission of *volentiers* is an error since this word is used three more times in the same paragraph and in each of these instances both Saint Pathus and Saint Denis reproduce it. The stylistic importance of *volentiers* is clear in the context of the whole paragraph:

> Chiers filz, *aies volentiers* la compaingnie des bonnes gens avecques toy, soient de religion, soient du siecle, et eschive la compaingnie des mauvez, et *aies volentiers* bons parlements avec les bons; et *escoute volentiers* paller de Nostre Seigneur en sarmons et en privé. *Pourchaces volentiers* les pardons.

Since the word *volentiers* is consistently used in this paragraph to reinforce the verb that it follows, the absence of the first *volentiers* in the Saint Denis and Saint Pathus texts implies that the word was also absent from the common (Latin) manuscript from which, we are led to believe, they both probably descend.

In paragraph fourteen we have the following reading in the *Noster* manuscript:

> Nulle parole qui tourt a despit de Nostre Seigneur ou de Nostre Dame ou des sains ne seuffre en nule maniere, que tu n'en praignes venjance.

In contrast to this reading, the Saint Denis and Saint Pathus texts mention Our Lord and the saints but not Our Lady. This omission takes on even greater importance in view of the fact that in paragraph twenty-eight Saint Louis makes a similar enumeration:

> Et met grant pene a ce que li pechiés soient ostés de ta terre, c'est a dire li vilain serement et toute chose qui se fait a despit de Dieu ou de Nostre Dame ou des sains...

and in this instance the two other versions are in accord with the *Noster* text. Thus, we see that in paragraph fourteen the *Noster* manuscript was probably correct in mentioning *Nostre Dame* in her rightful as well as traditional place between God and the saints, whereas the omission in the Saint Pathus and Saint Denis texts can only be explained by the faultiness of a common source.

Not only did the Latin prototype of the Saint Pathus and Yves texts make omissions from time to time, but it also added words or passages for the sake of clarity. In paragraph three, for example, the *Noster* manuscript reads: *Chiers filz, je t'enseigne premierement que*. In all likelihood the scribe who composed the Latin prototype of this paragraph wished to connect the first two introductory paragraphs with the third paragraph, i. e., with the first formal teaching, and in order to do this he introduced this paragraph with the phrase *propter hoc*. Saint Pathus rendered this *propter hoc* by the phrase *pour ce;* his text of the third paragraph reads: Pour ce, chiers filz, *je t'enseigne que...*

Paragraph twenty-seven of the *Noster* text is brief and to the point in saying:

> Chier filz, je t'enseigne que tu soies touz jours devoz a l'Yglise de Romme et a nostre pere l'Apostole,...

On the other hand the two other texts are obviously concerned with giving an even clearer version of this teaching. This concern, combined with their lexical and syntactic characteristics forces one to conclude that they are both derived from a common source, quite possibly the Latin text of the canonization inquest. The Yves of Saint Denis text, *tu sis semper devotus ecclesiae Romanae et summo pontifici patri nostro,* is clumsily translated back into French by Saint Pathus. He begins by rendering *summo pontifici* by *soverain evesque,* a questionable translation since there is a clear difference between the words *pontifex* (Pope) and *episcopus,* the Latin equivalent of *evesque*. Saint Pathus goes on to translate *nostri patri* as *nostre pere,* but he has qualms about the inexactitude of his rendering of *pontifici;* he feels obliged to add, for the sake of clarity, *c'est le pape*. Here are the three texts side by side; the *Noster* version is indeed free of Latinisms:

> NOSTER: et a nostre pere l'Apostole.
> S. DENIS: et summo pontifici patri nostro.
> S. PATHUS: et au soverain evesque, nostre pere, c'est le pape.

Textual comparisons such as these all point in the same direction, for they all indicate that the *Noster* manuscript contains a purely

French text of the Teachings whereas the Saint Pathus and Saint Denis texts are descendants of a common Latin ancestor.

Reference to the variants appended to the following text will indicate that there are a great many examples of textual agreement of the Saint Denis and *Noster* texts against that of Saint Pathus, whereas there are very few cases where Saint Pathus and *Noster* agree to the exclusion of Saint Denis.

In paragraph nineteen, for example, the *Noster* manuscript reads: "Sioes bien diligent de faire garder *en ta terre* toutes manieres de genz." The Saint Pathus text gives *par ton royaume*. Paragraph sixteen contains a similar example wherein the *Noster* reading, "Chiers filz, se il avient que tu viengnes *au royaume*," is in agreement with the Saint Denis text *ad regnum* against the Saint Pathus version *a regner*.

The meaning of this relationship only corroborates earlier conclusions. For the disagreement between the Saint Pathus and Saint Denis texts is caused by the fact that Saint Pathus' text is a translation of a Latin text or is based on one, while at the same time these very differences also indicate that Saint Pathus' Latin source could not be the Saint Denis text.

The ultimate source of the disagreement is Saint Pathus' desire to give a faithful translation of what he considers to be the meaning of the Latin and on many occasions we find him adding phrases for the sake of clarity. In paragraph ten, for example, he adds the phrase *et doies dire* to the *Noster* and Saint Denis reading *se ce est chose que tu puisses dire*. Likewise, in the middle of paragraph nineteen, *Noster* reads *Et il respondi*, which agrees with the Saint Denis text *ipse respondit*, while Saint Pathus amplifies: *Et adonques li diz rois Phelippes respondi en ceste maniere*.

The text contained in the *Noster* manuscript is therefore the one which most faithfully conserves Saint Louis' original. Like the two other texts of the long version, it certainly contains the spirit of Louis' Teachings and, since close study of the text has revealed that it contains no Latinisms, there is no reason to doubt that it also reproduces the letter of Louis' Teachings.

THE *NOSTER* MANUSCRIPT

Charles-Victor Langlois' 1899 study of the *Chambre des comptes de Paris* [1] showed that a list of the five original registers contained in the *Chambre des comptes* was made by Jean le Bègue in the fifteenth century and that these five registers were named, respectively, *Croix, Pater, Noster, Qui es in caelis* and *Saint-Just.* However, the fire of 1737 in the *Chambre des comptes* ostensibly destroyed all the archives. Langlois then discussed the Bibliothèque Nationale ms. lat. 12814, which contains the *Noster* text and proved beyond a shadow of a doubt that the *Noster* register had indeed survived:

> Nous sommes en mesure d'établir que *Noster* est le seul de tous les *Libri Memoriales* de l'ancienne Chambre des comptes qui n'ait pas été détruit. Il existe encore. C'est le manuscrit latin 12814 de la Bibliothèque nationale, dont on a eu tort de dire qu' "il ne figura jamais dans les dépôts de la Chambre" et qu "aucun inventaire n'en fait mention." Ce manuscrit, égaré au XVe siècle, retrouvé le 13 novembre 1465, a été égaré de nouveau à une epoque indéterminée, jusqu'à ce qu'il soit venu échouer à la Bibliothèque de Sainte-Geneviève-des-Prés en 1728. Il était en sûreté à la Bibliothèque de Sainte-Geneviève-des-Prés lorsque l'incendie de 1737 détruisit tous les autres Mémoriaux... Ainsi, *Noster*, dit aussi *Liber parvus viridis* ou Petit livre sans aiz, et le manuscript latin 12814 de la Bibliothèque nationale ne sont qu'un seul et même manuscrit. [2]

---

[1] Joseph Petit, *Essai de restitution des plus anciens Mémoriaux de la Chambre des comptes de Paris,* intro. Ch.-V. Langlois (Paris, 1899).

[2] *Ibid.,* pp. XII-XIII.

According to Langlois, the manuscripts in the *Chambre des comptes* go back as far as the thirteenth century and in this regard the text of the Teachings contained in manuscript B. N. 12814 is no exception. It dates from the end of the thirteenth or the beginning of the fourteenth century. Now since the holograph of Saint Louis was composed at about that time and since there are no traces of Latin influence in the manuscript, there is no reason to doubt that this manuscript contains a faithful reproduction of the holograph of Saint Louis.

Also supporting the validity of manuscript B. N. 12814, i. e., the *Noster* manuscript, is the fact that in 1627 Adam Théveneau [3] included in his biography of Saint Louis a text of the Teachings which he claimed reproduced the text to be found in the *Noster* register of the *Chambre des comptes*. This text was published more than a century before the fire that destroyed the *Chambre des comptes* in 1737, and, remarkably enough, it reproduces word for word, though in modernized seventeenth-century French, the text of the Teachings to be found in manuscript B. N. 12814. There is therefore no reason to doubt that the ancient *Noster* manuscript of the *Chambre des comptes* which contained "une énorme quantité de documents précieux pour l'histoire de France depuis le XIIIe siècle," [4] and the modern manuscript B. N. 12814 are actually one and the same thing.

This historical evidence only corroborates what textual analysis has already amply demonstrated: that the *Noster* manuscript (i. e., ms. lat. B. N. 12814) does indeed contain the most faithful copy available of Saint Louis' holograph of the Teachings to Philip.

Now to terminate this discussion of the *Noster* manuscript, let us recall André Artonne who in 1955, after giving the *étai présent* of the problems concerning Saint Louis' Teachings, called for a "mise au point définitive," stating that "les arguments de Levillain ne paraissent pas convaincants, mais ils n'ont pas été refutés." [5] Levillain noted, in comparing the *Noster* manuscript of the

---

[3] Adam Théveneau, *Les préceptes du roy saint Louis à Philippe III son fils* (Paris, 1627), p. 534.

[4] Petit, *op. cit.*, p. 1.

[5] André Artonne, "Le recueil des traités de Charles V," *Recueil de travaux offerts à Clovis Brunel*, I (Paris, 1955), 62.

Teachings to Philip with the versions of the Instructions to Isabelle found in both Gerard of Montaigu and B. N. 25462, certain linguistic and stylistic resemblances to him so impressive, that he felt bound to conclude that the *Noster* text of the Teachings to Philip never passed through Latin and hence must be a copy of Saint Louis' holograph. [6] But then, reasons Levillain, why are the texts of the Instructions to Isabelle (with the exception of the version of William of Saint Pathus) always accompanied by a short version of the Teachings instead of the long one?

In Levillain's view the long version of the Teachings was placed together with the Instructions to Isabelle in the *Trésor des chartes* by Philip III. However, during the reign of Philip the Fair, the short version of the Teachings — i. e., the one that omits the article on the Pope — was placed in the *Trésor des chartes* in place of the long one which, in turn, was remanded to the *Chambres des comptes*. Levillain explains the switch by supposing that, since the short version of the Teachings omitted the article calling for fidelity to the Pope, it suited Philip the Fair. And Philip hoped the short version would gain credence and authority by being put alongside the text of the Instructions. These, of course, make no mention at all of the Pope since Isabelle was not destined to become a head of state as was her brother Philip. Thus, in accordance with his political policies toward Innocent IV, Philip took care to see that the manuscript was carefully guarded — not in the *Trésor des chartes* with the text of the Instructions — but rather in the *Chambre des comptes* where Levillain probably assumed it would have been less in evidence.

Levillian then goes on to say that when Gerard of Montaigu discovered a text of the short version of the Teachings and the text of the Instructions (now to be found in register AA4 of the Bibliothèque Municipale d'Amiens), he immediately recognized the short version of the Teachings to be false, but he did consider the text of the Instructions to Isabelle to be Saint Louis' holograph. Levillain supports this interpretation by recalling the note that Montaigu appended to the text of the Teachings he had

---

[6] Léon Levillain, "Discours présentés à la Société de l'Histoire de France," *Annuaire-Bulletin de la Société de l'Histoire de France*, May 16, 1933, pp. 71-84.

discovered, i.e., the note describing the version as one "escripte d'une grasse lectre, qui n'étoit pas trop bonne." [7] Levillain would have us believe that the short version of the Teachings is false whereas the text of the Instructions found in the Montaigu manuscript is authentic. Therefore, since the *Noster* manuscript resembles this latter text (i.e. the Instructions to Isabelle) in a way which, unfortunately, he does not specify, he concludes that the *Noster* manuscript of the Teachings must contain the holograph of Saint Louis.

Now then, the *Noster* manuscript does indeed contain a text which brings us as close as possible to Saint Louis' original handwritten copy. But not only can we quarrel with Levillain's conclusions (he claims that the *Noster* manuscript actually contains the holograph of Saint Louis and not just the best available descendant of the holograph), his reasoning is, to say the least, dubious. For example: (a) Levillain simplifies matters somewhat. Letting aside the text by William of Saint Pathus, of the four texts of the Instructions to Isabelle which are accompanied by short texts of the Teachings to Philip, only two of these latter texts omit the article on the Pope whereas the other two retain it. By neglecting to mention this, but nevertheless proposing a textual substitution on the part of Philip the Fair, Levillain simplifies to the point of falsification. (b) Levillain's statement that the Montaigu manuscript and the B.N. manuscript 25462 of the Instructions to Isabelle use the same language and style as the *Noster* manuscript of the Teachings to Philip is purely impressionistic; he offers no example to support his contention. (c) Although the texts of the Instructions to Isabelle do share with the *Noster* manuscript a common lack of Latinisms, none of the texts of the Instructions agree perfectly among themselves. Furthermore, of the two manuscripts of the Teachings which Levillain mentions by number, B.N. 25462 and Amiens AA4, the text of the Instructions in the former is far superior to that of the latter which differs greatly from *Noster* in vocabulary. Levillain was obviously trying to prove that neither the *Noster* manuscript of the Teachings nor the text of the Instructions show any trace of Latin influence,

---

[7] *Ibid.*, p. 82.

but instead of demonstrating his point by a close study of the manuscripts, he merely speculated on their origin. (d) A final error of misinterpretation vitiates Levillain's explanation of the note attached to the copy that Montaigu had made of the manuscript he had found. The whole tenor of the note obviously implies that Montaigu was convinced that he had found the original copy of the Teachings. Otherwise he would not have brought it to the king (who, in turn, gave it to his own brother-in-law, Louis of Bourbon) before writing on the copy that he had put back in the *Trésor des chartes,* "L'original de ces Enseignemens lequel estoit escript d'une grasse lectre qui n'étoit pas trop bonne." The implication is clear and, until Levillain chose to see otherwise, all scholars had been in agreement on this point: Montaigu wrote the note because he mistook the poor hand of a *copiste* for the original handwriting of Saint Louis. Levillain's theory that Philip the Fair substituted the short version of the Teachings for the long one in the *Trésor des chartes* is therefore indefensible for it is nothing but pure speculation and rests on no tangible proofs.

But perhaps the fact that Levillain made his findings known in an oral *compte-rendu* instead of as a formal scholarly article explains why he did not bother to prove his major assertions. For if the text in the *Noster* manuscript is clearly not Saint Louis' holograph, it is nonetheless the best text available to us and doubtless reflects both the spirit and the letter of Louis' Teachings to his son Philip.

The evidence examined would seem to show that the holograph of Saint Louis gave birth to three manuscript traditions. They are 1) the abbreviated Latin translation by Geoffrey of Beaulieu; 2) the Latin translation which was made for the canonization investigation and of which both the Saint Pathus and Saint Denis texts are descendants; and 3) the integral French copy of Saint Louis' holograph which is represented by the text found in the *Noster* manuscript.

The accompanying stemma attempts to portray graphically the relationship existing among the various manuscripts of the Teachings. The Beaulieu text of the Teachings is the prototype of all the texts of the short version of the Teachings, whether or not they contain the controversial article on the Pope, as well as of the interpolated version. It also gave birth to the Latin text of William of Nangis and the various French texts which contain the short version, as well as to the texts of the Teachings that are found in Joinville and the *Grandes Chroniques de France,* although these latter texts have eliminated certain paragraphs from the Beaulieu text and added others which are to be found neither in the Beaulieu text nor in Saint Louis' holograph. The stemma also illustrates the relationship between the Saint Pathus and Saint Denis texts of the long version, both of which emanate from a Latin ancestor, whereas the *Noster* text contains no such adulteration and reflects both the spirit and the letter of Louis' Teachings.

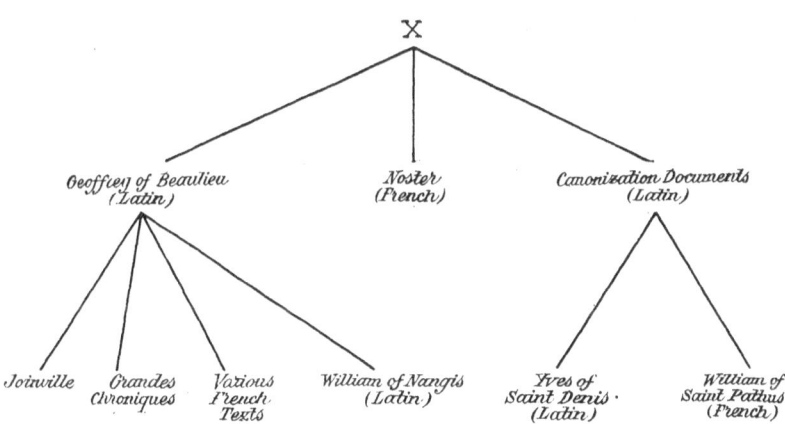

DATE OF COMPOSITION

It is impossible to say with any degree of certainty when the Teachings were composed or when they were passed on to Philip, for none of Louis' biographers supply this information. H.-Fr. Delaborde has proved conclusively [1] that both Joinville and the chroniclers who composed the *Grandes Chroniques* relied, when recording the events surrounding Louis' death, upon Geoffrey of Beaulieu who administered the last sacraments to the dying king. The Beaulieu text, reproduced above (p. 16) informs us that Louis wrote in French *(in Gallico)* and in his own hand *(manu sûa)*. He also states that the Teachings were left to Philip on the assumption that he would relay them to the other children *(et in ipso ceteris liberis)*. Unfortunately, he does not tell us when they were written or how they were communicated to Philip, saying only that the king left them *(reliquit)* to Philip. The problem is further complicated by the cryptic phrase *ante suam extremam infirmitatem* which ultimately tells us nothing for it could refer either to the period preceding Louis' departure for North Africa (June 1270), or to the brief amount of time he spent there before falling sick and dying.

In referring to the biographies of Saint Louis which contain the long version of the Teachings, namely the Saint Denis and Saint Pathus texts, we do not gain any further insights, for if Saint Pathus tells us that the Teachings were simply left *(lessa)* to Philip, [2] Saint Denis tells us that they were sent *(misit)*. [3]

---

[1] Henri-François Delaborde, "Le Texte primitif des Enseignements de saint Louis à son fils," *BECh*, LXXIII (1912), 76.
[2] Saint Pathus in *RHGF*, XX, 84.
[3] Saint Denis in *RHGF*, XX, 47.

In reviewing this rather sketchy evidence, the only definite conclusion that can be drawn is that the Teachings were given to Philip by his father *ante suam extremam infirmitatem,* and were delivered personally by the king and not sent. There is no reason to doubt that Beaulieu is telling the truth and, furthermore, being the king's confessor and an eye-witness at his death, he was as well-situated as anybody to know what happened. Given this lack of hard fact to go on, we can therefore assume, and it is nothing more than an assumption, that the Teachings were composed and bestowed upon Philip by his father at some time before their departure from France in June 1270. For one can hardly expect a king to have the time to conceive and write down with his own hand a long series of moralistic teachings while busily leading a military campaign in enemy territory.

Assuming that the Teachings were composed before June 1270, let it stand as the date *ad quem.* The date *a quo* at which Louis could have written and presented the Teachings to Philip is the year 1260 for in January of that year his oldest son Louis died, and Philip became the next in line to the throne. These two extreme dates can be narrowed down considerably if we take into account the fact that Philip was not knighted until the 5th of June 1267 when he was already twenty-two years old. This event in itself does not preclude the possibility that Louis might have given him the Teachings at an earlier date but, in the light of other events that took place in 1267 and 1268, it is improbable that the Teachings were composed and given to Philip before 1267.

Indeed, during a period lasting from March to June, 1267, Louis demonstrated great concern about the future of the kingdom, not only in terms of the succession of Philip III, but also with respect to the eventual liberation of the Holy Land. First of all, he ordered all the prelates and nobles of the kingdom to be in Paris at the middle of Lent which, in 1267, fell on March 24, the vigil of the Feast of the Annunciation. [4] On the following day, Louis announced his intention of setting out on another crusade and formally called upon all the leaders of the realm to take the cross then and there with him and his three sons. On

---

[4] Le Nain de Tillemont, *Vie de saint Louis* (Paris, 1847-1851), V, 14.

June 5 of the same year, Louis once again assembled all his vassals and prelates to attend the dubbing ceremony of his oldest son and successor, the future Philip III.[5] Philip, born on May 1, 1245, had been second in line to succeed his father until the death, in 1260, of his older brother Louis (born February 25, 1244). He had thus gone unknighted for twenty-two years, though, for seven years, he had been Louis' oldest son. This dubbing of Philip is not to be taken as a recognition of his majority for he had ceased to be considered a minor at the age of fourteen.[6] It might be interpreted however as a semi-official recognition of his son as future successor, as well, of course, as a formal bestowal of knighthood, which would allow him to participate legally in the upcoming crusade. It was also at this time that Louis chose to endow him with land for the first time, giving him Orléans, Châteauneuf-sur-Loire, and several other territories.[7]

In addition to preparing for the crusade, for which he started raising money on March 25, and regularizing his oldest son's position, Saint Louis also took advantage of the presence of his vassals and prelates in Paris to invite them to take part in another ceremony: on June 6, the day after Louis received his knighthood, Louis led a long procession outside the walls of the city to the Abbey of Saint Denis where, according to Le Nain de Tillemont, "il prit ... la résolution de faire changer les corps des rois enterrez dans cette église."[8] These events show that Louis was clearly giving considerable thought at this time to the problems of succession and tradition, both of which figure importantly in the Teachings.

In the light of this admittedly circumstantial evidence one might venture to conclude that the Teachings were composed sometime between March and June of 1267 and that they were given to Philip at a personal interview held during that four month period. In this case, the date *a quo* for the composition and bestowal of the Teachings on Philip would be on or about

---

[5] *Ibid.*, 34.

[6] Paul Viollet, *Histoire des institutions politiques et administratives de la France*, I (Paris, 1890), 88.

[7] Tillemont, V, 36.

[8] *Ibid.*, 35.

the 26th of March 1267, the date on which Louis revealed his plans for another crusade and on which he and his three sons formally took the cross. Nevertheless, there is still room for speculation here, for although the Teachings might well have been composed and passed on to Philip between March and June of 1267, the fact remains that Saint Louis waited almost an entire year — until February 1268 — before composing his will. It is unlikely, however, that Louis wrote the Teachings after composing his testament since, in that document, he makes no mention whatsoever of Philip or of the problem of succession, thereby hinting that perhaps the problem had already been taken care of. He does mention his sons John, born in 1250, Peter, born in 1251, and Robert, born in 1256, to whom he gives "certas terrarum portiones, secundum quod in litteris nostris patentibus super hiis conjectis plenius continetur," and his last child Agnes, born after 1256, to whom he gives "decem milia libras." [9] Yet he makes no provision whatsoever for his married daughters Isabelle, Marguerite, and Blanche, or for his oldest son and successor, Philip. If February 1268 is proposed, then, as the latest possible date *a quo* for the composition of the Teachings, this still represents nothing more than a calculated guess based on the king's activities concerning the succession during the previous year. But the facts of these circumstances do suggest that this would have been a likely period for him to compose the Teachings. One cannot, however, rule out the possibility, no matter how remote, that the Teachings still might have been composed after the will but before Louis' June 1270 departure for North Africa. Therefore, again for safety's sake, let us consider June 1270 as the extreme date *ad quem* for the composition and transmission of the Teachings, for it is quite unlikely that Louis would have found the time to compose the Teachings to Philip after he had left French soil.

---

[9] Saint Louis, "Epistola Publicata Super Obitu Ludovici Noni Regis," ed. Duchesne, *Historiae Scriptores Francorum*, V (Paris, 1649), 440.

SOURCES

Louis IX was a genuinely learned man, a characteristic he no doubt inherited from his close association with the clergy who zealously supervised (along with his Spanish mother, Blanche of Castille) his education as a youth. He read Latin as well as French and enjoyed spending his leisure hours reading aloud to his friends and close associates. Geoffrey of Beaulieu marvelled at his ability to jump back and forth between the two languages:

> Quando studebat in libris ei aliqui de familiaribus suis erant praesentes qui litteras ignorabant, quod intellegebat legendo, proprie et optime noverat coram illis transferre in Gallicum de Latino. [1]

As all of Louis' biographers tell us, he would gather these friends and relatives around him every evening "el tens d'entre disner et heure de dormir" [2] to exchange ideas and opinions about God, the saints, and their actions, as well as stories from sacred scripture and the lives of the Fathers. He also founded a library in the *Sainte Chapelle* where he put at the disposal of all those religious who would want to consult them, copies of the works which he considered to be of capital importance:

> Sicut cogitavit, ita et reversus perfecit, et locum aptum et fortem ad hoc aedificari fecit, scilicet Parisiis in Capellae suae thesauro, ubi plurima originalia, tam Augustini, Ambrosii, Hieronymi, atque Gregorii, necnon et aliorum orthodoxorum doctorum, libros sedule con-

---

[1] Geoffrey of Beaulieu in *RHGF*, XX, 15.
[2] Saint Pathus, in *RHGF*, XX, 79.

gregavit: in quibus quando sibi vacabat, valde libenter studebat, et aliis ad studendum libenter concedebat. ³

Louis' chief sources of inspiration and counsel, after the Bible, were the writings of the Fathers of the Church and the lives of the saints, "car il avoit la bible glosee, et originaux de saint Augustin et d'autres sainz, et autres livres de la sainte escripture." ⁴

Louis' reliance upon the Bible — especially upon sections of the Old Testament in which God speaks to the patriarchs and kings of their duties — was so total that almost every paragraph of the Teachings could be traced back to Scripture. The Bible can be considered then as an implicit source for all his thought, whereas other influences are somewhat more explicit, as for instance Saint Augustine. Saint Louis manifests a strong tendency to view the world from a point of view reminiscent of Augustine's early Manicheanism, and the whole tenor of the Teachings leans toward a dualistic view of the world and even of a constant struggle between the forces of good and evil, where the king is responsible for everything that happens in his kingdom. Error and sin are not to be tolerated, and for both Louis and Augustine the king must root out evil and establish the City of God where the forces of evil are dominated and eventually crushed. We are not certain whether or not Louis actually aspired to incarnate the ideal of the Christian emperor that Augustine put forth in his *De Civitate Dei,* but there is no reason to think that he was unaware of Augustine's proposed ideal.

Another area of possible influence that cannot be overlooked are the *Specula Regis,* two of which were written for and dedicated to him by leading philosophers of his day. The first of these is the *Eruditio Regum et Principum* ⁵ of Gilbert of Tournai, written in 1259, while the second, the *De Morali Principis Institutione,* ⁶

---

³ Beaulieu, in *RHGF,* XX, 15.
⁴ Saint Pathus, in *RHGF,* XX, 79.
⁵ Gilbert of Tournai, *Eruditio Regum et Principum,* ed. A de Poorter (Louvain, 1914).
⁶ As far as I know there is only one printed edition of this work: *De Morali Principis Institutione,* Rostochii, Fratres domus horti viridis, ca. 1476. Since this work has proved to be unobtainable, the reader is referred to Astrik Gabriel, *The Educational Ideas of Vincent of Beauvais,* University

was composed between 1260 and 1263 by Vincent of Beauvais. Each of these works is a veritable *floriligium* in which the authors quote, in addition to the Scriptures and the Fathers of the Church, an imposing number of authorities from pagan antiquity. Their purpose in both works is to advise the king on virtually every aspect of his private and public life, with the ultimate goal being the establishment of a just reign. In deciding the amount of importance that should be given to these works as possible sources for Louis' Teachings, it is essential to recall Geoffrey of Beaulieu's comment to the effect that the king "non libenter legebat in scriptis magistralibus, sed in sanctorum libris authenticis et probatis." [7] In the light of his distaste for the scholastics and his preference for reading directly from the scriptures, it is perhaps wise not to place too much emphasis on them as possible sources.

Vincent of Beauvais composed another compendium, dedicated to Louis' wife Marguerite, which treats specifically the education of the royal children. The *De Eruditione Filiorum Nobilium*, [8] written between 1247 and 1249, bears no relationship to the Teachings, for it is theoretical in nature, being intended to serve as a guide for the royal tutors. Louis was doubtless familiar with it, since he took a great interest in his children's education, but it certainly exercised little or no influence on his writing of the Teachings.

In Louis' family there were two mighty forces that contributed greatly to the formation of his thinking: his grandfather Philip Augustus and his mother Blanche of Castille. There are many examples scattered through the various biographies of Saint Louis that testify eloquently to his devotion to the memory of his grandfather, whom he especially revered for his force and authority in handling his vassals, and in his respect for the Church when she was acting within her bounds. For like Philip Augustus, Louis held firm against the Church on many occasions when it was necessary to do so to protect his legitimate interests. As for

---

of Notre Dame Texts and Studies in the History of Medieval Education, IV (Notre Dame, Ind., 1956), 43.

[7] Geoffrey of Beaulieu, in *RHGF*, XX, 15.

[8] Vincent of Beauvais, *De Eruditione Filiorum Nobilium*, ed. A. Steiner (Cambridge, Mass., 1938).

Queen Blanche, who directed the young king's steps through a stormy regency period, and then acted as monarch again during the six years he was absent on the Seventh Crusade, Louis always conserved a special affection for her, even to the point, as Joinville reminds us, of risking the neglect of his wife.

But of all the influences that must have exerted themselves upon this extraordinary king, the most important had to be the effect, over the length of a lifetime, of his vast experience. For Louis was much more than the pious soul that well-meaning hagiographers have created for us over the centuries. He was also a man of action and of strong passions, a fierce warrior in combat, a shrewd and cunning negotiator in ecclesiastical wranglings over Church property and benefices, and a gifted diplomat in handling the territorial disputes with England. His experiences were wide and varied, carrying him abroad at the head of two crusades, the first of which kept him away from France from 1248 to 1254 and the second finally claiming his life. And the impact of these six years overseas in a strange and hostile land must have exerted a strong and lasting effect on him, although we can not measure for sure exactly what that effect was. If we know, for instance, that the library that he founded in the *Sainte Chapelle* was inspired by a Moslem prince's library that Louis had inspected,[9] we can only guess at other undocumented oriental influences that may very well have been at work on Louis while he was composing his Teachings.

In summary, we see that the Teachings emerge on the one hand as a result of Louis' own personal reflections on the Bible (especially the Old Testament), the writings of the Fathers of the Church (especially Saint Augustine), and the advice given him by his close relatives, especially his mother and his grandfather. In addition, there were the many counsels offered him by the thinkers of his day who were close to him, among whom might have been Gilbert of Tournai and Vincent of Beauvais. On the other hand, there was the ever-present influence exerted upon him by the weight and breadth of his own experience, and the insight which came to him over the years as a result of that

---

[9] Beaulieu in *RHGF*, XX, 15.

experience. In this respect, his six-year sojourn in the Near East must have played an important, although undetermined role.

But when all these things are considered, the whole is greater than what seems to be the sum of its parts. For Saint Louis represents more than what we might try to erect as sources of his thought. At best, we can only point to possible influences and leave it at that. A man of Louis' genius and sanctity is more fully appreciated when allowed to speak for himself.

Text of the Teachings

CE SONT LES ENSEIGNEMENZ QUE MONSEIGNEUR SAINT LOYS FIST A SON AINSNE FILS PHELIPPE

1) A son chier filz ainzné Phelippe salut et amitié de pere. [1]

2) Chiers filz, pour ce que je desirre de tout mon cuer que tu soies bien enseignié en toutes choses, [2] je pense que je [3] te face aucun ensaingnement par cest escript; car je t'oÿ dire aucunes foiz que tu retendroies plus de moy que d'autrui.

3) Chiers filz, [4] je t'enseingne premierement que tu aimmes Dieu de tout ton cuer et de tout ton pouoir, car sanz ce nulz ne peut riens valoir. [5]

4) Tu te dois garder de toutes [6] choses que tu quideras qui li doient desplaire, a ton pouoir, [7] et especialment tu doiz avoir ceste volenté que tu ne faces pechié mortel pour nulle chose qui puist avenir, et que tu te lairoies avant touz les mambres tranchier et la vie tolir par cruel martire que tu le feïsses a escient.

5) Se Nostre Sire t'envoie aucune persecution ou de maladie ou d'autre chose, tu la dois souffrir debonnairement, [8] et l'en dois mercier et savoir bon gré; car tu doiz penser que il l'a fet pour ton bien. Et si doiz panser que tu as bien deservi et ce et plus, se il vousist, pour ce que tu l'as pou amé et pou servi et que tu as maintes choses faittes contre sa volenté.

6) Se Nostre Sire t'envoie aucune prosperité ou de santé de corps ou d'autre chose, [9] tu l'en doiz mercier humblement et doiz prendre garde que tu de ce n'empires ne par orgueil ne par autre mesprison; car c'est moult grant pechié de guerroier Nostre Seigneur de ses dons.

7) Chier filz, je t'enseigne que tu t'acoustumes a souvent confesser et que tu eslises touz jours telz confesseurs qui soient de saincte vie et de souffisent lettreüre, par qui [10] tu soies enseigniez des choses que tu doiz eschiver et des choses que tu dois faire, et aies tele maniere en toy par quoy ti confesseur et ti autre ami t'osent hardiement enseignier et reprendre.

8) Chier filz, je t'enseigne que tu oyes volentiers le service de sainte Esglise, et quant tu seras ou moustier, garde toy de muser et [11] de parler vainnes paroles. Tes orisons di en pez, ou par bouche ou par panser, et especialment soies plus en pez et plus ententiz a oroison tant comme li corps Nostre Seigneur Jhesu Crist [12] sera presens a la messe et une piece devant.

9) Chiers fils, je t'enseigne que [13] tu aies le cuer piteus envers les povres et envers touz ceus que tu cuideras qui aient meschief ou de cuer ou de corps et, selon le pouoir que tu avras, les sequeur volentiers ou de confort ou d'aucune aumosne.

10) Se tu as aucune mesaise de cuer, di la a ton confesseur ou a aucun que tu cuides qui soit loyaus et qui te sache bien celer, [14] pour ce que tu la portes plus en pez, se ce est chose que tu puisses dire. [15]

11) Chiers filz, aies volentiers [16] la compaingnie des bonnes gens avecques toy, soient de religion, soient du siecle, et eschive la compaingnie des mauvez, et aies volentiers bons parlemens avec les bons; et escoute volentiers paller de Nostre Seigneur en sarmons et en privé. Pourchaces volentiers les pardons.

12) Aime le [17] bien en autrui et hé le mal.

13) Et [18] ne seuffre mie que l'en die devant toy paroles qui peuent genz attraire a pechié. N'escoute pas volentiers mesdire d'autrui.

14) Nulle parole qui tourt [19] a despit de Nostre Seigneur ou de Nostre Dame [20] ou des sains ne seuffre [21] en nule maniere, que tu n'en praignes venjance. Se il estoit clerc ou il estoit grant personne que tu ne deüsses justicier, feïsses le dire a celui qui le porroit justicier.

15) Chiers filz, pren te garde que [22] tu soies si bons en toutes choses par quoy il appere que tu recognoisses les bontez et les honneurs que Nostre Seigneur t'a faittes en tele maniere que, se il plaisoit a Nostre Seigneur que tu venisses au fez et a l'onneur

de gouverner le royaume, que tu fusses dignes de recevoir la saincte unction dont [23] li roy de France sont sacré.

16) Chiers filz, se il avient que tu viengnes au royaume, [24] gardes que [25] tu aies les vertus qui affierent a roy, c'est a dire que tu soies si droituriers que tu ne declines [26] de nulle droiture pour nulle chose qui puit avenir. Se il avient que il ait aucune querelle d'aucun povre contre aucun riche, soustien plus le povre que le riche, jusques a tant que tu en saches la verité, [27] et, quant tu entendras la verité, fai le droit.

17) Et se il avient que tu aies querelle encontre aucun [28] autrui, soustien la querelle de l'estrange devant ton conseil, ne ne fai pas semblant d'amer trop ta querelle [29] jusques a tant que tu cognoisses la verité, car cil du conseil en pourroient estre doubtiz a parler contre toy, laquele chose tu ne doiz pas voloir.

18) Se [30] tu entenz que tu tiengnes riens a tort ou de ton temps ou du temps de tes ancesseurs, tantost le rent, [31] combien que la chose soit grant, ou en terre ou en deniers ou en autre chose. Se [32] la chose est obscure, par quoy tu n'en puisses savoir la verité, fai tele paiz par conseil de preudomes par quoy t'ame en soit du tout delivrée et l'ame de tes ancesseurs; et combien onques [33] que tu oyes dire que tes ancesseurs aient rendu, [34] met touz jours peine a savoir se riens y a encor a rendre, [35] et se tu le treuves, tantost le fai rendre pour la delivrance de t'ame et des ames de tes ancesseurs.

19) Soies bien diligent de faire garder en ta terre [36] toutes [37] manieres de genz et especialment les personnes de sainte Esglise; ceuz deffens, que l'en ne leur face tort [38] ne force, [39] ne en leurs personnes ne en leurs choses; et je te vueil ci recorder une parole que dist li roys Phelippe, mes ayeus, si comme un de son conseil me recorda, qui disoit que il l'avoit oÿe. Li roys estoit un jour avec son conseil privé, — et y estoit cil qui la me recorda, — et li disoient cil de son conseil que li clerc li fesoient moult de tort [40] et que l'en se merveilloit commant il le souffroit. [41] Et il respondi: [42] "Je croi bien que il me font moult de tort; [43] mès quant je pense aus honeurs que Nostre Seigneur m'a faittes, je vueil mieuz souffrir [44] mon dommage que faire chose par quoy il venist esclandre [45] entre moy et sainte Esglise." Je te recort ce pour ce que tu ne soies pas legiers a croire nullui contre les personnes de

sainte Ysglise; ainz les doiz honnorer [46] et garder si qu'il puissent faire le service Nostre Seigneur en pès.

20) Ainsi [47] t'anseigne je que tu especialment aimmes les genz de religion, et les sequeur volentiers a leur besoing; et ceus que tu cuideras par qui Nostre Seigneur soit plus honorez et servis, ceuz aime plus que les autres. [48]

21) Chiers filz, je t'enseigne que tu aimes ta mere et honores et que tu retiegnes volentiers et faces ses bons enseignemens et soies enclins a croire ses bons conseilz. [49]

22) Tes freres aimes et vueilles touz jours leur bien et leurs bons avancemens, et leur soies en leu de pere a euz enseignier a touz biens, mès gardes que, par amour que tu aies a nullui, ne declines de droit faire ne ne faces [50] chose que tu ne doies.

23) Chiers filz, je t'enseigne que [51] les benefices de sainte Ysglise que tu avras [52] a donner, que tu les doingnes a bones personnes par grant conseil de preudomes; et il me samble qu'il vaut mieux que tu [53] les doignes a ceuz qui [54] n'avront nules prouvendes que ce que tu les doignes aus autres; car tu trouveras assez de ceus qui riens n'ont, se tu les quiers bien, en [55] qui il sera bien emploiez.

24) Chiers filz, je t'enseigne que tu te gardes a ton pouoir que tu n'aies guerre a nulz crestiens et, se l'en te fait tort, [56] essaie pluseurs voies pour savoir se tu porroies trover voie par quoy tu peüsses recouvrer ta droiture avant que tu feïsses guerre, et aies entencion que ce soit pour eschiver les pechiez qui se font en guerre. Et se il avient qu'il la te couvigne faire, ou pour ce que aucun de tes hommes se defausist en ta court de droit prendre, ou que il feist tort a aucune yglise ou a aucune povre personne [57] ou a quelque personne que ce fust et ne le vousist amender par toy, ou pour autre cas raisonnable pour quelque chose que ce fust qu'il te couvenist a faire guerre, commande diligemment que les povres genz qui coulpes n'ont en forfet soient gardez que dommage ne leur viegne ne par arson [58] ne par autre chose; car il t'affiert mieux que tu contraignes le maufeteur par prendre les seues choses ou ses villes ou ses chastiaus par force de siege. Et garde que tu soies bien conseilliez, avant que tu meuves nulle guerre, que la cause soit moult raisonnable, et que tu aies bien sommé le maufetaur et tant atendu comme tu devras.

25) Chiers filz, je t'enseigne que les guerres et les contenz qui seront en ta terre ou entre tes hommes, que tu mettez pene de les [59] apaisier a ton pouoir; car c'est une chose qui moult plest a Nostre Seigneur; et mes sires saint Martin nous a donné moult grant exemple, car il ala pour mettre pais entre les clers qui estoient en son arceveschié, au temps qu'il savoit par Nostre Seigneur qu'il devoit mourir, et lui sembla qu'il metoit bone fin en sa vie en ce faire.

26) Chier filz, pren te garde diligemment que il ait [60] bons bailliz et bons prevoz en ta terre; et fai souvent prendre garde [61] que il facent bien droiture, [62] que il ne facent a autrui tort [63] ne chose que il ne doient. De ceus mesmes qui sont en ton hostel, fai [64] prendre garde que il ne facent a nullui chose que il ne doient, [65] car, ja soit ce que tu doies haïr tout mal en [66] autruy, tu doiz plus haïr le mal qui vendroit de ceus qui de toy avroient [67] le pouoir que tu ne doiz des autres, et plus doiz garder et deffendre qu'il n'aviegne. [68]

27) Chiers filz, je t'enseigne que tu soiez touz jours devoz a l'Yglise de Romme et a nostre pere l'Apostole, [69] et li portez reverence et honeur si comme tu doiz [70] a ton pere espirituel.

28) Chier filz, donne volentiers pouoir a genz de bonne voulenté qui en sachent bien user, et met grant pene [71] a ce que li pechié soient ostés en ta terre, c'est a dire li vilain serement et [72] toute [73] chose qui se fait ou dit a despit de Dieu ou de Nostre Dame ou des sains: pechiez de corps, jeu de dez, tavernes et les autres pechiez. Fai ce abatre en ta terre sagement et en bonne maniere. [74] Les hereges a ton pouoir [75] fai chacier de ta terre et les autres males genz, si que ta terre en soit bien purgiée, si comme tu entendras que il sera affaire par sage conseil de bonnes genz.

29) Les biens avances par tout ton pouoir; met grant pene a ce que tu saches recognoitre les bontez que Nostre Seigneur t'avra faitez et que tu l'en saches mercier. [76]

30) Chiers filz, je t'enseigne que tu metez grant entente a ce que li denier que tu despendras soient en bon usage despendu et que il soient pris droiturierement. [77] Et c'est un sens que je voudroie moult que tu eüsses, c'est [78] a dire que tu gardasses de foles mises et de mauveses prises [79] et que tes deniers feussent bien

pris et bien mis; [80] et cestui sens t'enseigne Nostre Sires [81] avec les autres sens qui te sont profitable et couvenable.

31) Chier filz, je te pri, que se il plaist a Nostre Seigneur que je trespasse de ceste vie [82] avant toy, que tu me faces aidier par messes et par autres oroisons et que tu envoiez par les congregations [83] du royaume de France pour faire demander leurs prieres [84] pour m'ame, et que tu entendes a touz les biens que tu feras que Nostres Sires m'i doint part.

32) Chier fils, je te doing toute la benoïçon que pere puet et doit donner a fil, et pri Nostre Seigneur Dieu Jhesu Crist que il, par sa grant misericorde et par les prieres [85] et par les merites sa benoite mere vierge Marie [86] et des anges et des archanges et de touz sains et de toutes saintes, que il te gart et te deffende que tu ne faces chose qui soit contraire a sa voulenté, et que il te doint grace de faire sa voulenté si que il soit serviz et honorez par toi, et face il [87] a moy et a toy par sa grant largece si que, après ceste mortel vie nous [88] puissons venir a lui a la vie pardurable la ou nous le puissons veoir, amer et louer sans fin. Amen.

33) A lui soit gloire, honeur et louange qui est un Dieu avec le Pere et [89] le Saint Esperit sanz commencement et sanz fin. Amen.

VARIANTS

The letter symbols indicate the following texts:
N = B. N. ms. lat. 12814.
N¹ = B. N. ms. fr. 5869.
N² = B. N. ms. fr. 4641^b.
P = text of Saint Pathus in RHGF, XX, 84-86.
D = text of Saint Denis in RHGF, XX, 45-47.

1. *P omits* amitié de pere.
2. *N* tout chos.
3. *N omits* je.
4. *P* Pour ce chier fuiz; *D* propter hoc care fili. *The* Noster *manuscript omits upon occasion the final s of chiers. Faithful to the principle of only changing the text when it is obviously incorrect, the final s, when absent, will not be reconstituted.*
5. *P* car sanz ce ne puet nul valoir nule chose; *D* quia sine hoc nullus potest.
6. *N* tout.
7. *D omits* (a ton pouoir).
8. *P* tu la dois souffrir de bonne volente; *D omits* (tu... debonnairement).
9. *P omits* ou de sante... chose; *D* ut corporis sanitatem vel aliam.
10. *N* par qy; *P* par lesquex; *D* per quos.
11. *N omits* et, *given by* PD.
12. *N omits* Jhesu Crist, *given by* PDN¹N².
13. *N adds* je t'enseigne que tu, *omitted by* PDN¹N².
14. *P* que tu saches que il te celera bien; *D* quod sciat te bien celare.
15. *P adds* et doies dire.
16. *PD omit* volentiers.
17. *N omits* le, *given by* PD.
18. *PD omit* Et. *In the* Noster *manuscript paragraphs twelve and thirteen read as one sentence and there is no logical* break. *Paragraphs sixteen and seventeen are comparable; there is continuity of thought between the two and the latter begins with* Et.
19. *P* puisse torner; *N²* tourne.
20. *PD omit* ou de Nostre Dame.
21. *N* celle ne seuffre.
22. *P* Pourvoi que; *D* provide quod.
23. *P* de laquele; *D* qua.
24. *P* a regner; *D* ad regnum.

25. *P* porvoi que; *D* provides quod.
26. *P* declines ne desvoies; *D* declines.
27. *P omits* jusques... verité; *D* quousque scias veritatem.
28. *P* encontre autrui; *D* aliquam habere querelam.
29. *P* ne ne montre pas que tu aimmes mout ta querele; *D* ut non ostendas te nimis diligere querelam tuam.
30. *P* Et se; *D* Et si.
31. *P* fai le tantost rendre; *D* fac statim restitui.
32. *P* Et se.
33. *P omits* onques.
34. *P* aient teles choses rendues.
35. *P* non porquant aies tozjors grant volenté de savoir se il demeure riens de ces choses a rendre; *D* adhibeas semper diligentiam ad sciendum si adhuc superest id ad reddendum.
36. *P* par ton royaume; *D* ex terra.
37. *N* tout.
38. *P* injure; *D* injuria.
39. *P* violence; *D* violencia.
40. *P* mout d'injures; *D* multas injurias.
41. *P* comment il pooit tele chose soufrir; *D* quomodo ipse sustinebat.
42. *P* Et adonques li diz rois Phelipes respondi en ceste maniere; *D* ipse respondit.
43. *P* asses d'injures; *D* multas injurias.
44. *N* faire; *P* soufrir; *D* sustinere.
45. *P* discorde; *D* scandalum.
46. *P* aincois leur porte enneur; *D* imo des eis honorem.
47. *P* et ausi; *D* similiter.
48. *P* et aime ceus plus que les autres que tu sauras qui plus ennorent Dieu et serviront; *D* et illos per quos putabis Dominum nostrum plus honorari et ei plus serviri dilige plusquam alios. *P is syntactically incorrect here.*
49. *P* a son bon conseil; *D* ad consiliis bonis ejus.
50. *P* fai as autres.
51. *N* que tu.
52. *P* tu as; *D* habebis.
53. *N* tu doignes; *D* offeras.
54. *N* et il me samble qu'il vaut mieuz que tu doignes a ceus qui riens n'ont; *P* et m'est avis que miex vaut que tu les doignes a cels qui n'avront nules prouvendes, que ce que tu les doignes aus autres, car se tu enquiers bien, tu trouveras assez de ceus qui riens n'ont; *D* et videtur mihi melius quod tu conferras illis qui nullas habebunt praebendas quam aliis si enim bene quaeris, satis invenies de illis qui nihil habent. *N seems to contain a* bourdon *here which is based on the words* ceus qui.
55. *N* a; *P* en; *D* in quibus.
56. *P* et s'il te fesoit aucunes injures; *D* et si fieret tibi injurias.
57. *P* autre persone; *D* aliqui personae. *Louis was most likely using the word* persone *here in the sense of clergyman.*
58. *D omits* (ne par arson).
59. *N* de l'apaisier; *PD construct the sentence differently.*
60. *P* tu aies; *D* sint.
61. *P* pourveoir; *D* provideri.

VARIANTS

62. *P* justice; *D* justitiam.
63. *P* injure; *D* injuriam.
64. *N* te fai.
65. *P omits* ceus... ne doient. *D seems to contain a* bourdon *here which is based on the word* debeant.
66. *N* a autruy; *P* en autre; *D* in alio.
67. *P* ont; *D* haberent.
68. *P* que ce n'aviegne que ta gent facent mal; *D* si contingat.
69. *P* et au souverain evesque nostre pere c'est le pape; *D* et summo pontifici patri nostro.
70. *P* tu dois fere; *D* sicut debes.
71. *P* et pense par grant diligence; *D* et adhibeas magnam diligentiam.
72. *N* en.
73. *N* tout.
74. *P* a ton pooir; *D* sapienter et bono modo.
75. *P* sagement et en bonne maniere; *D* pro posse.
76. *P* que tu l'en saches rendre graces; *D* et quod scias ei gratiari.
77. *P* et que il soient justement receuz; *D* et quod sint juste recepti.
78. *N* et est a dire; *P* c'est a dire; *D* hoc est dicere. *In paragraph twenty-eight the* Noster *manuscript reads correctly* c'est a dire.
79. *P* recettes; *D* receptionibus.
80. *P* bien mis et bien receuz; *D* bene missi et bene recepti.
81. *P* te voille Nostre Sires enseignier; *D* doceat te Dominus noster.
82. *P* que je parte de ce monde; *D* me decedere.
83. *P* par les congregacions des religions; *D* per sanctas congregationes.
84. *N* les demander par prieres; *P* requerre leurs prieres; *D* ad faciendum peti ab eis preces.
85. *N* la priere; *P* les prieres; *D* precibus.
86. *D omits* (sa benoite mere vierge Marie).
87. *P* et ce face Nostre Sires; *D* hoc faciat ipse.
88. *P omits* puissons venir a lui a la vie pardurable la ou nous le. *P seems to contain a* bourdon *here based on the word* puissons.
89. *P adds* et le Fiuz.

BIBLIOGRAPHY

Primary Sources:

BELLOLOCO, GAUFRIDUS DE (Geoffrey of Beaulieu). *Vita et Sancta Conversatio Piae Memoriae Ludovici quondam Regis Francorum*, in *Recueil des Historiens des Gaules et de la France*, ed. Bouquet *(RHGF)*, XX (1840), 3-27; also in *Historiae Francorum Scriptores (HFS)*, V (1649), 444-466.

JOINVILLE, JEAN DE. *Histoire de saint Louis, Credo et Lettre à Louis X*, ed. Natalis de Wailly, Paris, 1867.

NANGIOCO, GUILLELMOS DE. (William of Nangis). *Chronique latine* [Chronicon], ed. H. Geraud, 2 vols. Paris, 1843-1844; *Chronicon* also in *RHGF*, XX, 543-582.

SAINT-DENIS, YVES DE. *Gesta Sancti Ludovici Noni Francorum Regis*, in *RHGF*, XX, 45-57.

SAINT-PATHUS, GUILLAUME DE. *Les Miracles de saint Louis*, ed. P. B. Fay, Paris, 1931; also in *RHGF*, XX, 121-189.

―――. *Vie de saint Louis*, ed. H. Fr. Delaborde, Paris, 1899; also in *RHGF*, XX, 58-121.

Secondary Sources:

ARTONNE, ANDRÉ. "Le Recueil des Traités de Charles V," *Recueil de travaux offerts à Clovis Brunel*, Paris, 1955, 53-63.

BEAUVAIS, VINCENT OF. *De Eruditione Filiorum Nobilium*, ed. A. Steiner, Cambridge (Mass.), 1938.

BERGER, ELIE. *Histoire de Blanche de Castille, reine de France*, Paris, 1895.

DELABORDE, HENRI-FRANÇOIS. "Le Texte primitif des Enseignements de saint Louis à son fils," *BECh*, LXXIII (1912), 73-100.

―――. "Le Texte primitif des Enseignements de saint Louis à son fils," (suite et fin), *BECh*, LXXIII (1912) 237-262.

―――."Réponse de M. le comte François Delaborde," *BECh*, LXXIII (1912), 502-504.

DUCHESNE, FRANÇOIS. *Historiae Francorum Scriptores*, 5 vols. Paris, 1636-1649.

DUSEVEL, H. "Les Enseignements de saint Louis à son fils," *Annuaire-Bulletin de la Société de l'Histoire de France* (1939), 4-8.

GABRIEL, ASTRIK. *The Educational Ideas of Vincent of Beauvais*, University of Notre Dame Texts and Studies in the History of Medieval Education, IV, Notre Dame, Ind., 1956.

Langlois, Charles-Victor. *La Vie en France au moyen-âge*, IV, Paris, 1928, 23-46.

——. "Préface" to *Essai de restitution des plus anciens Mémoriaux de la Chambre des comptes de Paris*, Paris, 1889, I-XXII.

Levillain, Léon. "Discours présentés à la Société de l'Histoire de France," *Annuaire-Bulletin de la Société de l'Histoire de France* (1933), 71-84.

Le Nain de Tillemont. *Vie de saint Louis*, 6 vols. Paris, 1847-1851.

Paris, Gaston. "Compte-rendu," *Romania*, III (1874), 401-413.

Petit, Joseph. *Essai de restitution des plus anciens Mémoriaux de la Chambre des comptes de Paris*, intro. Ch.-V. Langlois, Paris, 1899, I-XXII.

Théveneau, Adam. *Les préceptes du roy saint Louis à Philippe III son fils*, Paris, 1627.

Thompson, James Westfall. *The Literacy of the Laity in the Middle Ages*, University of California Publications in Education, IX, Berkeley, 1939.

Tournai, Gilbert of. *Eruditio Regum et Principum*, ed. A. de Poorter, Louvain, 1914.

van Moé, Emile-A. *Les Enseignements de saint Louis*, Paris, 1944.

Viard, Jules, *Les Grandes Chroniques de France*, Paris, VII (1932), X (1953).

Viollet, Paul. "Note sur le véritable texte des Instructions de saint Louis à sa fille et à son fils Philippe le Hardi," *BECh*, XXX (1869), 129-148.

——. "Les Enseignements de saint Louis à son fils, *BECh*, XXXV (1874), 1-56.

——. "Les Enseignements de saint Louis à son fils, Lettre à M. le comte François Delaborde," *BECh*, LXXIII (1912), 490-501.

——. *Histoire des institutions politiques et administratives de la France*, 3 vols. Paris, 1890-1903.

Wailly, Natalis de. *Mémoire sur la langue de Joinville*, Paris, 1868.

——, "Mémoire sur le *Romant* ou Chronique en langue vulgaire dont Joinville a reproduit plusieurs passages," *BECh*, XXXV (1874), 217-248.

——. "Lettre à M. Gaston Paris sur le texte de Joinville," *Romania*, III (1874), 487-493.

www.ingramcontent.com/pod-product-compliance
Lightning Source LLC
Chambersburg PA
CBHW020422230426
43663CB00007BA/1282